MW00448023

Eight Favorite Duets
from The Great American Songbook

Contemporary Settings for Vocal Duet and Piano
Arranged by Mark Hayes

CONTENTS

CD Track Number/Title   Page

1. **Have Yourself a Merry Little Christmas** 3
   Words and Music by Hugh Martin and Ralph Blane

2. **I Got Rhythm** 10
   Music and Lyrics by George Gershwin and Ira Gershwin

3. **I'll Be Home for Christmas** 21
   Words by Kim Gannon, Music by Walter Kent

4. **Just One of Those Things** 27
   Words and Music by Cole Porter

5. **Over the Rainbow** 40
   Music by Harold Arlen, Lyrics by E. Y. Harburg

6. **Singin' in the Rain** 48
   Lyrics by Arthur Freed, Music by Nacio Herb Brown

7. **They Can't Take That Away from Me** 59
   Music and Lyrics by George Gershwin and Ira Gershwin

8. **You're the Top** 68
   Words and Music by Cole Porter

Performance Note

These duets may be performed by any combination of voices singing VOICE I and VOICE II. Feel free to customize these arrangements, singing different parts and even trading parts within a song.

Book (35535)	ISBN-10: 0-7390-7841-0	ISBN-13: 978-0-7390-7841-9
Accompaniment CD (35536)	ISBN-10: 0-7390-7842-9	ISBN-13: 978-0-7390-7842-6
Book & CD (35537)	ISBN-10: 0-7390-7843-7	ISBN-13: 978-0-7390-7843-3

All of the Mark Hayes arrangements in this collection are also available as choral octavos.

Please visit **alfred.com** or contact your favorite music dealer for more information.

Have Yourself a Merry Little Christmas

SATB	27339
SAB	27340
SSA	27341
TTBB	35780
SoundTrax CD	27342
SoundPax	27343

I Got Rhythm

SATB	25176
SSAB	25177
SoundTrax CD	25178
SoundPax	25179

I'll Be Home for Christmas

SATB	33190
SAB	33191
SSA	33192
TTBB	33193
SoundTrax CD	33194
SoundPax	33195

Just One of Those Things

SATB	31186
SAB	31187
SSAA	31188
SoundTrax CD	31189
SoundPax	31190

Over the Rainbow

SATB	27333
SAB	27334
SSAA	27335
TTBB	27336
SoundTrax CD	27337
SoundPax	27338

Singin' in the Rain

SATB	33179
SAB	33180
SSA	33181
2-part	33182
SoundTrax CD	33183
SoundPax	33184

They Can't Take That Away from Me

SATB	28772
SAB	28773
SoundTrax CD	28774
SoundPax	28775

You're the Top

SATB	33185
SAB	33186
SSA	33187
SoundTrax CD	33188
SoundPax	33189

1. HAVE YOURSELF
A MERRY LITTLE CHRISTMAS

Arranged by
MARK HAYES

Words and Music by
HUGH MARTIN *and* **RALPH BLANE**

have your-self a mer-ry lit-tle Christ-mas now.

have your-self a mer-ry lit-tle Christ-mas now.

Here we are as in old-en days, hap-py gold-en days of

Here we are as in old-en days, hap-py gold-en days of

yore. Faith - ful friends who are dear to us gath-er

yore. Faith - ful friends who are dear to us gath-er

near to us once more, once more.

near to us once more, once more.

Through the years we all will be to-geth-er if the fates al-

Through the years we all will be to-geth-er if the fates al-

low. Hang a shin-ing star up-on the high-est

low. Hang a shin-ing star up-on the high-est,

2. I GOT RHYTHM

Arranged by
MARK HAYES

Music and Lyrics by
GEORGE GERSHWIN
and **IRA GERSHWIN**

16

35535

3. I'LL BE HOME FOR CHRISTMAS

Arranged by
MARK HAYES

Words by **KIM GANNON**
Music by **WALTER KENT**

4. JUST ONE OF THOSE THINGS

Arranged by
MARK HAYES

Words and Music by
COLE PORTER

5. OVER THE RAINBOW

Arranged by
MARK HAYES

Music by **HAROLD ARLEN**
Lyrics by **E. Y. HARBURG**

Lyrics: When all the world is a hope-less jum-ble and the rain-drops tum-ble all a-

6. SINGIN' IN THE RAIN

Arranged by
MARK HAYES

Lyrics by **ARTHUR FREED**
Music by **NACIO HERB BROWN**

52

51 **Lively 2-beat feel** (♩ = ca. 120)

Why am I smil - in', and why do I sing?

Lively 2-beat feel (♩ = ca. 120)

Why does De - cem - ber seem sun - ny as spring?

109

Doo - va doot doo doo - va doo - va doot doo. Doo - va doot doo doo - va

rain,_____ sing - in' in the rain,_____

112

doo - va doot doo, the rain!_____

_____ the rain!_____

7. THEY CAN'T TAKE THAT AWAY FROM ME

Arranged by
MARK HAYES

Music and Lyrics by
GEORGE GERSHWIN
and **IRA GERSHWIN**

The way you wear your hat,

The way you wear your hat,

love.   Still I'll   al - ways, al - ways keep the   mem - 'ry   of

love.   Still I'll   al - ways, al - ways keep the   mem - 'ry   of

The way you hold   your knife,

the way we danced   till three,

the way you changed   my   life,___

the way you changed   my   life,___

No, no! They can't take that a - way from me!____ No, they can't take that a -

No, no! They can't take that a - way from me!____ No, they can't take that a -

way from me!

way from me!

8. YOU'RE THE TOP

Arranged by
MARK HAYES

Words and Music by
COLE PORTER

About the Arranger

Mark Hayes is an award-winning concert pianist, composer, and arranger of choral, vocal, piano, and orchestral music. With over 700 published works to his credit, Mark is well-known for his unique settings, which draw from diverse styles such as gospel, jazz, pop, folk, and classical to achieve a truly "American sound." He has recorded numerous solo piano albums and tours internationally as a concert artist and clinician.

A graduate of Baylor University, Mark is a recurring recipient of the Standard Award from ASCAP. He has produced and arranged over 50 recordings for various artists and publishers. *I've Just Seen Jesus*, a recording he orchestrated and produced, won the prestigious Dove award from the Gospel Music Association, which is the equivalent to a Grammy in gospel music. Mark has also been honored to conduct performances of his works at Carnegie Hall, Lincoln Center, and the Southwest ACDA Regional Convention.

For more information on Mark, please visit his website: **markhayes.com**.

Vocal Collections arranged by Mark Hayes

Please visit **alfred.com** for more information on these exceptional collections.

7 Praise and Worship Songs for Solo Voice
7 Psalms and Spiritual Songs for Solo Voice
8 Favorite Duets from The Great American Songbook
8 Favorite Solos from The Great American Songbook
10 Christmas Songs for Solo Voice
10 Folk Songs for Solo Voice

10 Hymns and Gospel Songs for Solo Voice
10 Spirituals for Solo Voice
Seven by Series:
   Seven by Gershwin
   Seven by Mercer
   Seven by Porter

Mark also has arrangements featured in the following vocal collections:

12 Folk Songs for Solo Singers
Encores for Solo Singers
Folk Songs for Solo Singers, Volume 2
Great Hymnwriters (Portraits in Song)
Great Spirituals (Portraits in Song)
Spirituals for Solo Singers, Volume 2
Spotlight Solos